simply romantic

D0724127

COFFEE
dates
FOR COUPLES

FamilyLife Publishing®
Little Rock, Arkansas

Coffee Dates for Couples
FamilyLife Publishing®
5800 Ranch Drive
Little Rock, Arkansas 72223
1-800-FL-TODAY • FamilyLife.com
FLTI, d/b/a FamilyLife®, is a ministry of Campus Crusade for Christ, Inc. (known as Cru in the U.S.A).

© 2013, 2015 FamilyLife

ISBN: 978-1-60200-712-3

FamilyLife®, FamilyLife Publishing®, and Simply Romantic® are registered trademarks of FLTI.

Cover image: © Stocksy.com/Gillian Van Niekerk

Printed in the United States of America

Second Edition

20 19 18 17 16   1 2 3 4 5

CONTENTS

CAUTION:

Hot contents! Coffee and conversation can reach a boiling point. Allow contents to cool. Sip carefully. Practice patience and understanding as you connect with each other.

COFFEE TALK 101

Acidity

The sharp, lively quality characteristic of high-grown coffee,
tasted mainly at the tip of the tongue. The brisk, snappy quality
that makes coffee refreshing.

Americano

A shot or two of espresso that has been poured into a glass filled
with hot water. Brewed coffee, only stronger.

COFFEE TALK 101

Arabica

Common name for Coffea arabica, one of the two
principle commercial species of coffee. Arabica accounts for
approximately 70 percent of world coffee production. Arabica is
the bean most used as "specialty" and "gourmet."

Aroma

The fragrance of coffee, either as roasted beans or brewed.

COFFEE ON THE GO

Advice for Her: Start the conversation
in the car on the way to the coffeehouse.
Many men open up more when they
don't have to make eye contact.

Hit the coffee shop in the local shopping mall
and browse the stores.

Gals, as you shop, ask him to choose
clothes he thinks you would look good in. Guys,
then let her make a few suggestions for
your wardrobe as well.

Visit a bookstore with a coffee shop.
Get cozy in the travel section.

Husbands, ask your wife to describe her dream
vacation: location, activities, length of stay, etc.
Now, wives, it's your turn to listen.

Pick up a cup of "joe" on your way
to a home improvement store.

Walk the aisles and describe your dream
home to each other, husbands going first this
time. When you're through, skim the home
improvement books, noting features to
add to your wish list.

This might seem a little strange, but try it anyway. Fill a thermos with hot coffee and head over to the nearest cemetery.

As you read the epitaphs, ask,
"What would you want said about you at
your funeral? For what character
trait do you want to be known?"

Here's one for the holidays:
With your coffee, gloves, and loved one to
keep you warm, walk (or drive) through
neighborhoods festooned with
Christmas lights.

Talk about which holiday you enjoy the most
and the ways you like to celebrate it.

Pick up your favorite gourmet
coffee on your way to the park. Then,
on the swings or seesaw, ask your love
these questions:

"What is your fondest childhood
memory? Who was your favorite relative?
And your favorite toy was . . . ?"

COFFEE TALK 101

Barista
A professional maker of coffee beverages;
employee of a coffee bar.

Blending
The art of combining two or more coffees,
usually to achieve a consistent flavor profile.

COFFEE AT HOME

At home watching television . . .

Every time you see coffee on
the tube or hear the word, you must
kiss. If you see steam, create some
of your own.

At home under the stars . . .

Talk about the five most important
milestones you've reached together.
Why are they important to you?

At home in the kitchen . . .

After serving coffee just the
way he or she likes it, sit down and ask,
"What do you look forward to today?"
Then really listen.

At home in the living room . . .

Settle in with mugs of hot java
and your wedding album. Take turns
talking about your favorite memories
from your special day.

At home during the holidays . . .

Turn on the coffee pot,
turn down the lights, put on
some Christmas music,
and enjoy the peace and quiet.

At home in bed . . .

When you know you're free
to sleep late the next morning, brew a
pot of the leaded stuff to keep you up
late. Start a long list of the things that
you find sexy in your spouse. Follow
up with visual aids and
demonstrations!

COFFEE TALK 101

Body
Coffee taster's perception of the weight, richness, and thickness of the flavor. Also referred to as "mouthfeel."

Café au lait
A traditional French drink made with equal portions of brewed coffee and steamed milk.

COFFEE TALK 101

Cappuccino

A coffee beverage made from espresso and
steamed milk, capped with milk foam.

Complexity

A quality of coffee that gives multiple taste sensations.

COFFEE TALK 101

Earthy

A flavor sometimes desired, more often not,
caused by less-than-optimal processing, giving coffee the
taste of dirt. Frequently found in Indonesian coffees.

Espresso

A concentrated coffee beverage made by forcing
water under pressure through finely ground coffee.
Used for making a variety of exotic coffee drinks.

COFFEE OFF THE BEATEN PATH

All-night diner

Cozy up in the kitsch of an all-night diner. Over your bottomless cups of joe, swap stories about the strangers who come and go, explaining to each other what keeps them up at this late hour.

Upscale restaurant

As you sip your espresso and finish
dessert, decide to which charity you
would give $100,000—pretending
that you had the money to give.

High school sporting event

Ask each other, "To what were you most committed in high school— music, schoolwork, sports, boy-friend/girlfriend, friends, car, work, family, or a club/group?"

Out-of-town coffee shop

Discuss where on earth
you would most like to meet
for coffee. Choose a city or region
on each continent.

Your in-laws' house

Arrange to have coffee with your in-laws.
While sipping your coffee, play footsie
with your spouse. Don't laugh—at least
while you're at the table.

Homeless shelter

Volunteer to serve coffee at a nearby
homeless shelter. Take time to talk to a
resident and learn part of his or
her life story.

COFFEE TALK 101

Frappuccino

A coffee slush, blending iced coffee,
milk, flavorings, and ice.

French Roast

A coffee (not necessarily from France) that has been
roasted so as to bring out the oils in the beans.
This process gives the finished product
a somewhat bittersweet flavor.

COFFEEHOUSE CONVERSATIONS

Cozy up in the corner of your favorite
coffeehouse and connect over each of
these conversation starters.

If a movie were made about your life,
whom would you like to play the lead role?
Why?

If you could have any super power,
what would it be? Why?

Create a fun date on a $10 budget.
Note your ideas on a napkin and plan for later.

How do you imagine God?
In your mind, what does heaven
look like?

Of all the items that have been
or are in production today, which would
you like to have invented? Why?

If you were forced to give up
one of your five senses, which would you
choose to lose—sight, hearing, touch,
taste, or smell?

If you were a car, what type of car would you be and why? In life, which gear are you in—reverse, neutral, drive, or overdrive?

Tell your spouse what he or
she did that won your heart.
Explain why it worked.

Gals, order the beverage most like
your hubby. Is he hot, strong, and
straightforward? Then drink black coffee.
As you make your comparisons,
be sure he (and no one else) notices
how you lick the edge of your cup.

Fact: Coffee has been scientifically linked to improving sexual functions in men and women.

COFFEE TALK 101

Froth
Thick, foamy milk. The result of steam aeration.

Fruity
A flavor that reminds the taster of fruit,
this quality is generally considered an asset.

COFFEE TALK 101

Italian Roast

Definition varies by region. Considered the darkest
roast to people on the East Coast of the United States,
as compared to French roast, which is considered
darkest to those on the West Coast.

Latte

A beverage created by mixing espresso and steamed milk.
May or may not be topped off with milk foam.

COFFEE AROUND THE WORLD

ITALY
Coffea

Find a quaint little Italian restaurant
and enjoy a *coffea* and dessert.
Discuss: Which Italian city would you
most like to visit—Rome, Florence, Milan,
Naples, or Venice? Why?

HAWAII
Kope

While enjoying a cup of *kope*, plan a dream vacation to Hawaii. Now figure out how you can make your dream a reality.

GREECE
Kafes

In Greece, the eldest is customarily
served *kafes* first. Take turns naming
and describing adults from your youth
who had an impact on your life.

JAPAN
Koohii

The Japanese are known to
bathe in coffee grounds fermented
with pineapple pulp. Consider
sipping *koohii* together in a
coffee-scented bubble bath.

FRANCE
Café

On July 12, 1789,
Camille Desmoulins called his fellow
citizens to arms while standing on a
table in the Café de Foy coffeehouse.
Two days later the French Revolution
began. If you could change one
thing in the world today,
what would it be?

ETHIOPIA
Buni

Ethiopia is the birthplace of coffee.
In five minutes or less, tell your
spouse everything you remember
about your birthplace.

COFFEE TALK 101

Macchiato

Italian for "marked." Foamed milk on top of an
ounce-and-a-half of espresso. Served in a demitasse.

Mellow

Having well-rounded flavor that results when sugar combines
with the salts in coffee, causing a slightly sweet sensation.
Hawaiian Kona coffee is considered mellow.

COFFEE QUESTIONS AND QUIZZES

Wives, how would you describe your husband's
personality using these coffee terms?

hot	fresh
robust	soft
sweet	strong
spicy	creamy
delicate	mild
smooth	unique
nutty	balanced
mellow	wild

Husbands, how would you describe your wife's
personality using these coffee terms?

hot	fresh
robust	soft
sweet	strong
spicy	creamy
delicate	mild
smooth	unique
nutty	balanced
mellow	wild

Of the following accessories to your coffee ritual,
which is nonnegotiable?

☐ travel mug
☐ coffeemaker with timer
☐ cash for coffeehouse visits
☐ cup holder in my car
☐ creamer/sugar
☐ other

Of the following accessories to your relationship,
which is most important to you?

☐ hugs
☐ kisses
☐ cuddling
☐ making love
☐ listening
☐ encouragement
☐ gifts
☐ acts of kindness
☐ quality time together

If you could travel through time,
which of these historical coffeehouse events
would you attend? Why?

1732
The debut performance of Johann Sebastian Bach's
famous *Coffee Cantata* is given at a
coffeehouse in Germany.

1761
One hundred fifty stockbrokers meet at
Jonathan's Coffee House to form a club which
will later become the London Stock Exchange.

1776
The Declaration of Independence is read to
the public for the first time at the Merchant's Coffee House
in Philadelphia, Pennsylvania.

Here is a famous coffee slogan: "The best part of wakin' up is Folgers in your cup." What is the best part of waking up for you and your spouse?

Finish this acrostic of your sweetie's
best character qualities:

My wife is . . .	My husband is . . .
C_____	C_____
O_____	O_____
F _____	F _____
F _____	F _____
E _____	E _____
E _____	E _____

Which coffee blend best describes you as a lover?

Jamaican Blue Mountain: full bodied and smooth
Peaberry's Special: bright, bold, juicy, and rare
Mocha Java: complex and full bodied

Which coffee blend best describes you as a lover?

Breakfast Blend: bright, light bodied, and mild
Italian Roast: intense, full bodied, robust, and spicy
Costa Rica Reserve: deep, pungent, with a hint of smokiness

COFFEE TALK 101

Mocha

A latte with chocolate syrup added. May be topped with
whipped cream and cocoa powder or shaved chocolate.

Nutty

Having a flavor that reminds the
coffee taster of almonds or other nuts.

COFFEE TALK 101

Robusta

About 30 percent of the coffee grown in the world is robusta.
The scientific name is *Coffea canephora*. Usually less acidic and
aromatic than Arabica, sometimes bitter.

Solo

A single shot of espresso.

COFFEE TALK 101

Tone

The color of brewed coffee (e.g., light or dark toned).

Woody

Having an unpleasant wood-like taste.

COFFEE WARM-UPS

Coffee has two virtues. It is wet and it is warm.
–Old Dutch saying

Brew some steamy, stimulating
conversation with these more *intimate*
questions . . .

Which physical characteristic do
you most admire in your spouse? Why?
Be sure to give it special attention before
turning out the lights.

As a couple, what do you wish you had more time for? Talk about ways to carve time in your schedule.

How can you show more love and
respect to your spouse?

Talk about your sex life. Share what
you enjoy, ask how you can improve it,
and find out what your spouse wishes
you would or wouldn't do.

Would it be harder for you to give
up chocolate, coffee, or sex? Answer
honestly! Of the three, which two are
the best together? Try a sample.
(HINT: extra point for bringing
chocolate-covered coffee beans
to the bedroom!)

Think back to your first cup of coffee together.
Where were you and what brought you together?

What is that certain something your
spouse does that really turns you on?
Tonight, experiment and add another
"something" to each other's list.

What board game or video game
best describes your love life?

How can you turn your coffee dates
into foreplay?

When is the ideal time for sex? Life too crazy?
Take a few minutes to plan for some romance.

Who usually takes the initiative in the bedroom?
Figure out how to reverse the roles once in a while.

Coffee Memories

Best cup of coffee ever _____

Worst cup of coffee ever _____

Strangest place you've ever had coffee _____

Favorite coffee shop _____

Coffee Memories

Most romantic place to drink coffee _____

Best mood music for good coffee _____

Best time of day for coffee _____

Best coffee-drinking activity _____

Café Borgia
makes 4 servings

2 cups strong Italian coffee
2 cups hot chocolate
whipped cream
grated orange peel

1. Mix coffee and hot chocolate.
2. Pour into mugs.
3. Top with whipped cream and orange peel.

Turkish Coffee
makes 4 servings

1 1/2 cups cold water
4 teaspoons dark roast coffee (ground very fine)
4 teaspoons sugar

1. Heat water in saucepan, add coffee and sugar when warm.
2. Bring to boil.
3. Pour half of the coffee into demitasse cups.
4. Return remaining coffee to stove, and allow to return to boil.
5. Spoon off foam, and gently place into each cup (don't stir).

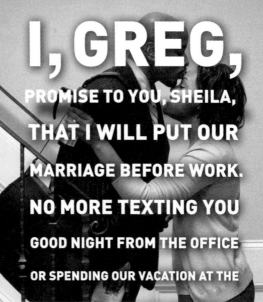

I, GREG,

PROMISE TO YOU, SHEILA,

THAT I WILL PUT OUR

MARRIAGE BEFORE WORK.

NO MORE TEXTING YOU

GOOD NIGHT FROM THE OFFICE

OR SPENDING OUR VACATION AT THE

FAN THE FLAMES OF ROMANCE!

Tips to Romance Your Husband and *Tips to Romance Your Wife* bring spark and sizzle to your marriage. Learn to communicate heart to heart, express love through food and fun, give gifts that say, "I love you!" and romance your love on birthdays and holidays. Heat up your marriage with these creative ideas and become *Simply Romantic!*

Shop.FamilyLife.com • 1-800-FL-TODAY